Crustaceans, What & Why?
Preschool Science Series

BABY PROFESSOR
EDUCATION KIDS

Crustaceans are arthropods ,
related to insects
and myriapods.

Crustaceans are animals that usually have a hard covering or exoskeleton, and two pairs of antennas, or feelers.

Crustaceans are the most diverse animal group in underwater habitats.

Shrimp, crabs, lobsters, barnacles and hermit crabs are all crustaceans.

Crustaceans don't have a skeleton; their hard exoskeleton protects their body and supports them.

The body of a crustacean is composed of body segments, which are grouped into three regions, the head, the thorax, and the abdomen.

Exoskeleton must be periodically molted when the animal undergoes metamorphosis.

Hermit crabs can't make their own shells. They hide in shells left behind by other animals.

Crabs live in all the world's oceans, in fresh water, and on land.

Hermit crabs are omnivores, which means they eat plants as well as meat.

Lobsters have poor eyesight, but have highly developed senses of smell and taste.

Lobsters have teethlike structures in their stomach, which grind partially digested food.

Lobsters carry their young for nine months.

The Japanese spider crab (Macrocheira kaempferi) is the largest crustacean in the world.